UNDERSTANDING THE HUMAN ELEMENT: HOW SOCIAL PSYCHOLOGY SHAPES CRIMINAL JUSTICE

By

DENISE N. FYFFE

Understanding the Human Element: How Social Psychology Shapes Criminal Justice

Copyright © 2007, 2023 by Denise N. Fyffe

Second Edition

Published in the United States by Jamaica Pen Publishers.

All rights reserved.

No part of this publication may be reproduced, stored in a retrieval system, or transmitted in any form or by any means (electronic, photocopying, recording, or otherwise) except with written permission of the publisher and in accordance with the provisions of the Copyright, Designs, and Patents Act 1988.

Book design by Jamaica Pen Publishers

PRINTED IN THE UNITED STATES OF AMERICA

Jamaica Pen Publishers
Maryland, USA.

www.jamaicapenpublishers.com/publishing

Table of Contents

Introduction 11
Understanding the Intersection of Theory and Practice 15
   Unlocking the Relationship between Social Psychology and Criminal Justice 15
      The Importance of Fairness in Criminal Justice 19
      The Goals of Criminal Justice 19
      The People Involved in Criminal Justice .. 20
      The Training and Skills Required for Criminal Justice Professionals 20
      The Challenges and Shortcomings of Criminal Justice 21
      Continuing Efforts to Improve Criminal Justice 21
      The Importance of Striving for True Criminal Justice 22
The Case 25
   Case Analysis 27
      Janis: Exploring Groupthink Theory 28
      Maslow's Needs Hierarchy 31

    Festinger: Deindividuation 34

    Triplett: Social Facilitation 35

    Bystander Effect 36

Nature vs. Nurture: The Debate on the Origins of Criminal Behavior 39

  Warr: Peer Influence on Delinquency 41

  Moffitt: AL & LCP Types of Delinquents ... 42

    Life-Course Persistent Delinquents 43

    Adolescent-Limited Offenders 43

  Warr: Status Striving and Delinquency 44

  Sociological Theories 44

  Subculture Theory 46

  Social Psychological Theory 47

    Risk Factors 48

The Roots of Crime: Examining the Complex Interplay of Biological, Sociological, and Social Psychological Factors 53

  Grid Iron Gang: Using Football as a Tool for Rehabilitation 54

    The Story of a Young Bully 54

    The Power of Teamwork 54

    Positive Changes in Attitude and Behavior 55

The Role of Applied Social Psychology in
Criminal Investigations and Prosecutions.........57
　Police Investigation.......................................57
　　Enhancing the Accuracy of Police
　　Investigations 59
　Police Interviews...60
　　Creating a Psychological Environment.....61
　　Social Dynamics 61
　　Interpretation of Behavior 62
　　Identifying Factors Affecting the Interview
　　Process 62
　　Key Variables to Distinguish Productive
　　Interviews from Unproductive Ones..........64
　　Employing Good Interviewing Techniques
　　..64
　　Creating the Right Environment for Each
　　Interviewee..65
　Line-up Identification 66
　　Reducing Eyewitness Errors through
　　Improved Line-up Procedures....................66
　　Factors that Influence Witness
　　Identification Accuracy.............................67
　　Reducing Eyewitness Misidentification....68

- Selection of Foils 68
- Informing the Witness 68
- Sequential Line-up 69
- The Courtroom 69
- Defense Lawyers 70
- Prosecutors 72
- Application of Social Psychology 74
- Juries 77
- The Prison Setting 82
- Purpose 84
- Types of Prison 86
- Attributes of Prison Workers 88

Criticisms of the System 93
- Lengthy Court Process 93
- Juvenile Delinquents 94
- Immoral Court Cases 94
- Insensitive Behavior 94
- Media as a Whipping Stick 95
- False Sense of Morality 95
- Corruption 96
- Hopelessness of Rehabilitation 96
- Negative Perception of Lawyers 97
- Unfair Judgments 97

- Negative Attitudes of Law Officers..............97
- Complacency 98
- Inability to Prevent Crimes 98

Positives of Social Psychology 99
- Improving Investigations 99
- Promoting Rehabilitation............................100
- Reducing Recidivism Rates 100
- Assisting Defense Attorneys.......................101
- Improving Jury Selection............................102
- Identifying Sources Of Bias And Error 102

Conclusion 105
References...109
Acknowledgment 117
Author Bio 118
Recommended Books 119
Dear Reader 123

UNDERSTANDING THE HUMAN ELEMENT: HOW SOCIAL PSYCHOLOGY SHAPES CRIMINAL JUSTICE

Introduction

Criminal justice and psychology are deeply interconnected fields that work in tandem to understand, prevent, and address criminal behavior. Criminal behavior is a complex social act that often arises from a variety of factors, including individual and social circumstances, cultural norms, and systemic inequalities. Understanding why people engage in criminal behavior is critical to building effective prevention and intervention strategies that promote safer and more just communities.

In this exploration of the intersection between criminal justice and social psychology, we will examine a range of theories that seek to explain and justify criminal behavior. From Festinger's cognitive dissonance theory to Maslow's hierarchy of needs, these theories offer insights into the underlying motivations and social pressures that contribute to criminal behavior. We will also explore the concept of groupthink and its role in shaping collective attitudes and decision-making processes that can lead to criminal behavior.

Another critical aspect of the criminal justice system is the way it interacts with and affects individuals and communities. Sociological theories of deviance, for example, can help us understand how certain behaviors come to be defined as criminal and how this definition can impact marginalized communities. Through case studies and real-world examples, we will examine the ways in which criminal justice policies and practices can both perpetuate and exacerbate systemic inequalities.

Ultimately, the goal of this exploration is to highlight the importance of a holistic and interdisciplinary approach to criminal justice. By drawing on the insights and expertise of multiple fields, including psychology, sociology, and law, we can build a more nuanced and effective understanding of criminal behavior and develop interventions that promote positive social change. Join me on this journey as we delve into the fascinating world of criminal justice and psychology, exploring the complexities of human behavior and the systems that seek to shape and control it.

Through this exploration, we will also delve into the role that psychology plays in the criminal justice system, from investigating and prosecuting criminal behavior to working with offenders to promote rehabilitation and reintegration into society. We will examine the ethical considerations involved in this work, as well as the challenges and opportunities that arise when applying psychological insights to real-world criminal justice contexts.

Finally, we will explore the ways in which advances in technology and research are shaping the future of criminal justice and psychology. From predictive policing to emerging neuroscientific research on criminal behavior, we will consider the potential benefits and risks of these developments and the ethical considerations that must be considered as we move forward.

Overall, this exploration will offer a comprehensive and engaging look at the intersection of criminal justice and psychology. It will highlight the importance of a multidisciplinary approach to examining, understanding and addressing criminal behavior in today's complex and rapidly changing world.

Understanding the Intersection of Theory and Practice

Criminal justice is a complex field that includes the study of criminal law, social control, criminology, victimology, and constitutional law. It also encompasses the loose array of institutions and activities, including policing, courts, corrections, and community services that make up a system. However, to fully comprehend the negative effects of crime and find ways to counter them, criminal justice must incorporate social psychology.

Unlocking the Relationship between Social Psychology and Criminal Justice

If you're wondering how social psychology is related to criminal justice, you're not alone. This topic has become a subject of interest for many researchers, students, and practitioners in recent years. To begin our exploration, we need to define some key terms and lay the groundwork for our discussion.

One essential concept is applied social psychology, which draws on theories, principles, methods, and research evidence to understand and address social and practical problems. According to Schneider et al. (2005), this branch of psychology looks at the nature of social psychological theory and how it can be used to enhance our understanding of social issues.

Another critical term is criminal justice, which encompasses the study of penal law, social control, constitutional law, criminal procedure and evidence, criminology, victimology, and various institutions and activities that make up the system, such as policing, courts, corrections, and community services. It also involves politics and the idea of administering justice.

To fully grasp the relationship between social psychology and criminal justice, we need to examine how crime operates. As Hoge (2001) noted in Schneider et al. (2005), crime is a function of interaction among multiple forces that operate at the individual, immediate social environment, and larger social environment levels. Therefore, criminal justice must incorporate social psychology to counter the negative effects of crime and fully understand its ramifications.

By understanding the fundamentals of applied social psychology and criminal justice, we can begin to see how they intersect and how social psychological theory can inform our approach to addressing criminal behavior. With this foundation, we can explore the ways in which social psychology is applied in the criminal justice system and its potential for creating more just and effective outcomes.

Criminal justice is the multifaceted application and study of laws related to criminal behavior. Those engaged in this field include law enforcement officers, judicial officials, lawyers, and advocates for systemic change. The aim of the criminal justice system is to deliver justice that is both fair and just. However, this goal is not always achieved due to the inherent flexibility in the application of laws, the interpretation of those laws, and the potential for laws to be unfair or biased.

Individuals who work within the criminal justice system, such as police officers and lawyers, receive specialized training to carry out their duties in a legal and ethical manner. For example, law enforcement officers are taught how to apprehend suspects while staying within the boundaries of the law. However, despite such training, there are still instances of injustice, such as when laws appear to be particularly unjust towards marginalized communities, who may have less access to quality legal representation.

The criminal justice system has a vital role in delivering justice for victims of crime, as well as ensuring that those who are accused of committing crimes are treated fairly. There is always room for improvement within this field, and many individuals continue to work towards the goal of true criminal justice, exemplifying fairness in their work and advocating for systemic change.

The Importance of Fairness in Criminal Justice

The criminal justice system exists to maintain law and order and ensure that those who break the law are held accountable for their actions. But beyond the enforcement of the law, it is important that criminal justice is also fair. The idea of justice is that everyone, regardless of their background or circumstances, is treated equally under the law. It is only through fairness that trust and confidence in the criminal justice system can be maintained.

The Goals of Criminal Justice

The ultimate goal of criminal justice is to maintain a safe and just society. This involves punishing those who break the law, deterring future criminal behavior, and rehabilitating offenders to prevent them from committing further crimes. The criminal justice system aims to achieve these goals through a range of measures, including policing, courts, and corrections.

The People Involved in Criminal Justice

Criminal justice involves a range of professionals, including police officers, judges, lawyers, probation officers, and correctional staff. Each of these professionals plays a critical role in maintaining law and order and ensuring that those who break the law are held accountable. Effective communication and collaboration between these professionals is essential to ensure that the criminal justice system operates efficiently and effectively.

The Training and Skills Required for Criminal Justice Professionals

Criminal justice professionals require a range of skills and training to perform their roles effectively. Police officers, for example, need to be physically fit, mentally resilient, and able to handle high-pressure situations. Lawyers must have strong analytical and communication skills and be able to apply complex legal principles to specific cases. A deep understanding of the law and an ability to apply it fairly is essential for all criminal justice professionals.

The Challenges and Shortcomings of Criminal Justice

Despite the best efforts of criminal justice professionals, the system is not always perfect. There are numerous challenges and shortcomings, including overcrowding in prisons, racial bias, inadequate resources, and corruption. These issues can undermine public trust in the criminal justice system and make it difficult to achieve the goals of maintaining law and order.

Continuing Efforts to Improve Criminal Justice

In response to these challenges, many individuals and organizations are working to improve the criminal justice system. This includes efforts to reform sentencing laws, reduce recidivism, and address racial and social inequality in the system. By striving to improve criminal justice, we can create a more fair, just, and effective system for all.

The Importance of Striving for True Criminal Justice

The criminal justice system is an essential component of a just and equitable society. While the system is not always perfect, it is important that we continue to work towards achieving true criminal justice. By prioritizing fairness, maintaining effective communication between criminal justice professionals, and addressing the challenges and shortcomings of the system, we can create a system that is more just, effective, and equitable for all.

Social psychology plays an important role in understanding and addressing the challenges and shortcomings of criminal justice. For example, social psychology research can provide insights into how biases and stereotypes impact decision-making in the criminal justice system, and how these biases can lead to unfair outcomes for certain groups. By understanding the psychological mechanisms behind these biases, criminal justice professionals can work to develop interventions that mitigate their effects and promote more equitable outcomes.

Additionally, social psychology can inform the training and skills required for criminal justice professionals. By studying social psychological principles and theories, criminal justice professionals can better understand how to communicate effectively with suspects and witnesses, how to build rapport and trust, and how to deescalate potentially volatile situations.

They can also gain insights into how to navigate complex social dynamics, such as power imbalances and cultural differences, which are often present in criminal justice settings. Ultimately, integrating social psychology into the training and skill development of criminal justice professionals can help to promote more effective and just outcomes.

The Case

Schneider et al. (2005) present a heart-wrenching case that showcases the complexities of criminal behavior and human nature. The case involves Dimitri "Matti" Baranovski, a 15-year-old high school student from Toronto, who was brutally attacked and killed in a park by a group of older teens.

The details of the case, including the possible reasons behind the attack and the bystander effect observed among those who witnessed the attack but failed to intervene, raise important questions about the factors that contribute to criminal activity. This case is not only a tragic story of a young life cut short, but also an opportunity to delve deeper into the interplay of genetics, sociological influence, and social interaction in criminal behavior.

> *"The evening of November 14, 1999, Dimitri 'Matti' Baranovski, a 15-year-old high school student from Toronto, sat with about six friends in the Harryetta Gardens playground in a park near their school and not far from where Matti lived with his*

mother. They often would come to the park to talk, socialize, and just hang out.

At approximately 8:45pm, they were approached by a group of 10 to 12 older teens and were asked whether they had any cigarettes or money. The intruders were wearing balaclavas over their faces so that their identities were not readily apparent.

When Matti and his friends told them they had no cigarettes or money, the young men persisted in their demands. At this point, Matti stood up against the group and told the older teens to stop bothering him and his friends. The details of what happened next are not entirely clear.

According to newspaper reports, three of the young men began to punch and kick Matti about his face and body. Matti's friends fled, leaving him alone with his assailants. As a result of the attack, Matti fell to the ground as they continued to brutally hit and kick him. One kick caused Matti's head to snap back, tearing an artery in his neck and killing him. The attack lasted a few minutes, after which the assailants fled.

One of Matti's friends had run across the street to a residence to summon help. The first 9-1-1 call came in at 9:02 pm (Wong, 1999). By the time the paramedics arrived on the scene, Matti's body was lifeless. Although he was revived later at the hospital, Matti died during the early morning hours of the next day.

It was later revealed that the young men had apparently come to the park looking for a fight with another group whose members failed to show up. They then turned their attention to Matti and his friends and decided to rob them. It also was revealed that at least two cars had passed by the scene that evening on the busy street that runs by the park. The drivers, on hearing Matti's screams, had slowed down or even stopped. In all cases, no one came to assist Matti or called for help.

According to one newspaper report (Wong, 1999), a woman driving by stopped her car when she and her two sons, who were passengers in the car, heard the noises from the attack. They reported hearing a loud cry for help and a lot of Russian words, followed by someone yelling "Get to the ground!" At that point, the woman, fearing that there might be weapons involved, became scared, and drove off."

Case Analysis

This case is a goldmine of information that we can use to explore different theories. Imagine a group of young men committing a heinous crime, and you might wonder what could have led them to do such a thing. Well, theories from great minds like Maslow, Janis, and Festinger could help us understand their actions.

Festinger's cognitive dissonance theory, for example, suggests that people strive to maintain consistency between their beliefs and actions. But when they act in ways that contradict their beliefs, they experience psychological discomfort. Applying this theory to the young men who committed the crime, it's possible that they experienced effort justification dissonance. This occurs when people engage in an activity that seems favorable at the time, but later question if it was worth the effort. To justify the action, they focus on the effort they put in rather than the outcome. In the case of the young men, the outcome may not have been positive, but the benefits to the gang's reputation and status in the community could have made the effort seem worthwhile.

Janis: Exploring Groupthink Theory

If we examine the case of Matti's murder and apply Janis's groupthink theory, it sheds some light on the group dynamics that led to this heinous crime. Janis's theory suggests that groupthink can occur when high group cohesiveness, structural problems, and situational pressure are present.

Matti's murder occurred when he challenged and stood up to the gang, leading to a situation where the gang members were under the influence of situational factors such as frustration and aggression. This situation, coupled with the gang's desire to defend its 'street cred' and respect, resulted in a poor decision to beat Matti to death.

Janis's theory helps us understand the group dynamics that led to this decision. When group cohesiveness is high, individuals are less likely to voice dissenting opinions or challenge the group's decision. Structural problems within the group, such as a lack of diversity in ideas or leadership, can also contribute to groupthink. Finally, situational pressure, such as the need to make a quick decision or to conform to group norms, can further exacerbate the effects of groupthink.

By applying Janis's theory to the case of Matti's murder, we can see how these three factors were present in the gang's decision-making process. However, it is important to note that groupthink is not an excuse for the gang's actions. Rather, it is a tool that can help us understand how group dynamics can lead to poor decision-making and even violence..

Understanding the Frustration Aggression Hypothesis and Conformity in Group Decision-Making

The frustration aggression hypothesis and conformity are two important concepts that shed light on the group decision-making process in the case of Matti. According to the frustration aggression hypothesis, individuals may become aggressive when their attempts to achieve a personal goal are thwarted. In this case, the gang's desire to maintain their reputation and street credibility may have been frustrated by Matti's refusal to comply with their demands. This frustration, coupled with the presence of potential victims (Matti and his friends), may have heightened the gang's aggression and led to the fatal outcome.

Furthermore, Janis' theory of groupthink suggests that individuals may conform to the decisions of the group, even if it goes against their personal values or judgment. This conformity can lead to poor decision-making, as seen in the case of the gang's decision to beat Matti to death. The group's failure to consider alternative options may have been a result of their cohesiveness and pressure to maintain their group identity and reputation.

It is important to understand these concepts to prevent such tragic events from happening in the future. By promoting individual thinking and encouraging alternative perspectives in group decision-making, we can avoid the pitfalls of groupthink and mitigate the negative effects of the frustration aggression hypothesis..

Maslow's Needs Hierarchy

This is a theory developed by Abraham Maslow that explains human motivation and behavior. According to Maslow, humans have a set of basic needs that must be fulfilled in order to achieve self-actualization, or the realization of one's full potential. These needs are arranged in a hierarchical order, with the most basic physiological needs such as food, water, and shelter at the bottom, followed by safety needs, social needs, esteem needs, and self-actualization needs at the top. Maslow's theory suggests that individuals must fulfill each level of needs in order to progress up the hierarchy towards self-actualization.

The Need for Social Acceptance and Group Formation

Humans have always been known to be social beings who desire to belong and be accepted by others. According to Maslow's hierarchy of needs, this need for belonging leads people to form social groups. However, this need for social acceptance can also lead to the phenomenon of groupthink, where individuals conform to the opinions and decisions of the group, even if it goes against their personal beliefs.

The Animal Instinct in Humans

Interestingly, animals also form social groups for the purpose of hunting and attacking their prey. This instinct to form groups for safety and protection is not exclusive to animals, as humans exhibit this behavior as well. In fact, joining a gang or group may provide individuals with the confidence and security to attack their victims, which would be difficult for one person to do alone.

Gangs and Security

In the case of Matti, the gang may have formed to ensure their security and protection. Attacking Matti and his friends in the park would have been risky for an individual to do alone, as their life would have been in danger. However, by forming a gang, they were able to protect themselves and attack their victims without fear of retaliation.

Overall, the need for social acceptance and the instinct for safety and protection can lead individuals to form social groups such as gangs. This can also lead to the phenomenon of groupthink, where individuals conform to the group's opinions and decisions, even if it goes against their personal beliefs.

Festinger: Deindividuation

The theory of deindividuation was first proposed by the American social psychologist Leon Festinger in 1952. Deindividuation refers to a psychological state where individuals lose their sense of individual identity and begin to act in a more impulsive or aggressive manner as part of a group. This phenomenon is often seen in situations where individuals are in large groups, wearing masks or uniforms, and where they feel anonymous. This can lead to a loss of self-awareness and can sometimes cause people to behave in ways that they would not otherwise.

In the case of Matti, the gang members who attacked him may have experienced deindividuation as they were wearing masks to conceal their identities, and this could have made them more likely to act aggressively and violently as part of the group..

Triplett: Social Facilitation

The concept of social facilitation was first proposed by Norman Triplett, a psychologist, in 1898. He observed that cyclists performed better when they were racing against each other rather than against the clock. This led him to believe that the presence of others can enhance performance on certain tasks. Since then, social facilitation has been extensively researched and the effects of social presence on human behavior have been observed in various settings.

Social facilitation is a psychological phenomenon where people tend to perform better on simple or well-rehearsed tasks when they are being watched by others, rather than when they are alone. This phenomenon is supported by a study conducted by Zajonc (1965) where he found that the presence of an audience could lead to increased performance on a simple task.

In Matti's case, social facilitation could have influenced the behavior of the gang members as they were performing a task that they had likely done before (i.e., attacking someone). Also, the presence of eyewitnesses could have further aroused them to perform better. However, social facilitation alone does not fully explain the extreme violence displayed in the attack. Rather, it is a complex interplay of multiple factors such as deindividuation and conformity.

Bystander Effect

The bystander effect theory was first proposed by social psychologists Bibb Latané and John Darley in 1968 following the murder of Kitty Genovese in New York City. They conducted a series of experiments to investigate why individuals were less likely to intervene or help in an emergency situation when other bystanders were present.

The bystander effect refers to the phenomenon in which people are less likely to help in an emergency situation when other bystanders are present. This phenomenon is often explained by a diffusion of responsibility, whereby individuals feel less personally responsible to intervene in a situation when others are present.

According to Schneider et al. (2005), the presence of other bystanders can decrease an individual's sense of responsibility to act. The decision to intervene is also influenced by the number of bystanders present and the similarity between the victim and the bystander. In Matti's attack, the presence of other bystanders may have played a role in their decision not to intervene.

The bystander effect, as highlighted by Darley and Latane (1968) and Latane and Nida (1981), can also come into play in emergency situations where individuals may not offer assistance due to the perceived ambiguity of the situation or the perceived similarity of the victim to the potential helper. These factors can lead to a diffusion of responsibility where individuals believe that someone else will step in and help, resulting in inaction. It is important to understand these factors and work towards addressing them to promote a more helpful and empathetic society.

Nature vs. Nurture: The Debate on the Origins of Criminal Behavior

The origins of criminal behavior have long been a subject of debate among criminologists and psychologists. While some argue that criminal behavior is a result of a person's genetic makeup, others believe that it is influenced by their environment and upbringing. But is it really a case of nature versus nurture?

Let's explore the interplay between biological, sociological, and social psychological theories to gain a better understanding of the roots of criminal behavior. Biological theories suggest that genetics, psychophysiology, neurological functioning, and biochemistry play a role in criminal behavior. Studies have shown that males, for instance, are more prone to aggression due to varying testosterone levels, especially when they are children of criminal parents.

While biological factors may influence a person's susceptibility to criminal behavior, sociological theories suggest that social and cultural factors also play a role. The environment in which a person grows up, including their family dynamics, peer groups, and socio-economic status, can shape their attitudes towards crime. Social psychological theories, on the other hand, suggest that the behavior of others, such as peers or authority figures, can influence an individual's decision to engage in criminal behavior.

The nature versus nurture debate is crucial in the criminal justice system as it shapes our approach to punishment, rehabilitation, and prevention efforts. By understanding the complex interplay between nature and nurture, we can develop more effective interventions to prevent criminal behavior and promote a safer society..

Warr: Peer Influence on Delinquency

Mark Warr's Companions in Crime: The Social Aspects of Criminal Conduct is a well-reasoned and well written account of the social influence of peers on crime and delinquency. It is one of the most comprehensive and sophisticated sociological treatments of peer influence on antisocial behavior. Warr's explanations for peer influence range from the most general (we are a gregarious social species) to the very specific (fear of ridicule, diffusion of responsibility, the anonymity of the gang, and status striving).

Warr's primary thesis is that association with delinquent peers causes delinquency. He clearly favors the causal role of delinquent peers over the alternative. He believes that the literature he reviews "supports the proposition that peer influence is the principle proximate cause of most criminal conduct". Antisocial behavior during adolescence is actually statistically normal; it is the youth who is consistently non-delinquent who is abnormal.

Adolescent antisociality has been observed for centuries. Plato commented on the unruliness of youth in his day in the Republic, and Shakespeare does likewise in The Winter's Tale. The problem is worse in the modern United States than in ancient Athens or Elizabethan England because of what Terrie Moffitt (1993) has termed "the maturity gap," as Warr (p. 130) points out. The maturity gap is that block of time, which can be as long as 10-12 years today, between puberty and the acquisition of socially responsible roles. The maturity gap was much shorter in days gone by when puberty arrived later, and socially responsible roles came earlier.

Moffitt: AL & LCP Types of Delinquents

The theory of life-course persistent (LCP) and adolescent-limited (AL) offenders was proposed by Terrie Moffitt, a psychologist and criminologist who is known for her work on developmental psychology and criminology. In the study of delinquent behavior, researchers have identified two distinct types of delinquents: life-course persistent (LCP) and adolescent-limited (AL) offenders.

Life-Course Persistent Delinquents

LCP offenders, as described by Moffitt in 1993, begin offending before puberty and continue well into adulthood. These individuals are believed to have heritable neuropsychological and temperamental impairments that result in negative interactions with others and lead to ever-hardening antisocial attitudes and behaviors.

Adolescent-Limited Offenders

In contrast, AL offenders do not have these impairments and are adequately socialized, having built up a store of social capital before adolescence. They are essentially pro-social youths who are temporarily derailed by the biological and social upheavals of adolescence. Effective parenting and positive responses from parents, teachers, and peers can help prevent these youths from becoming delinquent.

Warr: Status Striving and Delinquency

Warr writes at length about the importance of status, prestige, and respect within the adolescent group, status striving in groups "seems to be a feature of all primate species". There is something in the biology of all primates that leads them to seek status in groups. Status striving is thus part of our evolutionary baggage (an adaptation), and this evolutionary view of such efforts go a long way to helping us understand why young males often risk physical injury, or even death, to confront someone over the most trivial of insults to their claim to respect, especially males in so-called "honor subcultures" (Walsh, 2002).

Sociological Theories

So how does socio-economic status influence criminal behavior? Sociological theories are traditional theories, which have long sought to explain crime in relation to various factors in society such as social class, poverty, and social inequity. Thus, a person's socio-economic status, which is oftentimes determined by education, occupation, income, and neighborhood characteristics, explains substantial variability in criminal behavior.

They hypothesize that lower socio-economic status is associated with a higher rate of crime. It is believed that people who are from a lower socio-economic status are more likely to commit an offence. For example, according to strain theory by Cohen, (1960) as cited in Schneider et.al. (2005), criminal behavior is said to be caused by undue strain (frustration) experienced as a result of pathological social structures (e.g., social inequality, poverty) that prevent a person from achieving the middle-class expectations for material success. The strain leads the person to engage in socially deviant behavior, such as crime, to attain goods and social prestige.

Subculture Theory

The sociological Subculture theory, proposed by Wolfgang and Ferracuti (1981), suggests that individuals involved in criminal activities are following the hedonistic, hostile, and destructive values that are prevalent in the lower-class culture. Therefore, in poor countries one could speculate that reason why there are such high levels of crime is due in part to the low socio-economic status that exists within the inner-city communities and the subculture of having 'Dons' who create their own laws often times going against the laws of the country.

Essentially, the subculture theory states that there are a number of varied subcultures that people are affiliated with, and if they do not conform they are considered deviants of that particular culture. Indeed, in the deviant subculture, the nonconformists who do not engage in theft, drug use, and gang affiliation are said to be the true deviants (Andrews & Bonta, 2003 as cited in Schneider et al, 2005).

Social Psychological Theory

The social psychological theory of criminal behavior considers both dispositional and situational factors in explaining and predicting an individual's behavior. This theory considers various aspects, such as biological tendencies (such as temperament and attitude), environmental factors, and social interactions with others, to better understand and control criminal behavior. By considering all these factors, this theory provides a comprehensive framework for explaining and predicting the actions of individuals who engage in criminal behavior..

According to Bandura's (1977b) social learning theory, criminal activity represents learned behaviors that develop throughout a person's interactions and experiences with the social environment. This learning takes place as a result of various processes, including observing and imitating the criminal behavior of others, receiving positive consequences for engaging in criminal behavior (e.g., peer approval), realizing that such behavior can effectively lead to desired outcomes (i.e., have instrumental value), and developing a high sense of self-efficacy in using antisocial means to achieve one's aims (Schneider, et. al, 2005).

It is the work of Bandura that formed the foundation for the development of other sociological theories such as the general personality and social psychological model, developed by Andrew and Bonta (2003). They suggest that "the likelihood that a person will develop a tendency to engage in criminal behavior is increased by the presence of risk factors in his or her life.

Risk Factors

Six categories of risk factors—some personal and some environmental—are proposed:

- Onset of antisocial behavior at an early age
- Negative parenting and family experiences (e.g., harsh and abusive

discipline, low family cohesion, parental criminality)

- Volatile and personal characteristics that are conducive to criminal activity (e.g., impulsivity, aggressive energy, weak problem- solving abilities)
- Low levels of school or vocational achievement
- Association with pro-criminal peers and isolation from non-criminal associates
- Antisocial attitudes, values, and beliefs

Andrew and Bonta (2003) did not only examine individual factors in isolation but also considered socialization and peer interactions that may have contributed to parental and temperamental factors. They adopted a developmental approach that considered both positive and negative influences from infancy to the present. They investigated each of these influences and how they may have influenced an individual's susceptibility to engage in antisocial behavior, which can vary depending on the stage of development.

During the developmental stage, various factors, such as the family and peers, have a different degree of influence. The family, particularly during infancy, can significantly shape a person's character, attitude, and temperament. Research has shown that the formative years are crucial in a person's life, as they can influence their predisposition to antisocial people and criminal activities.

Consequently, individuals who are inclined towards criminal behavior are more likely to seek out groups and activities that offer the necessary support and reinforcement. According to Schneider et al. (2005), a person's likelihood of committing an offense increases if they value antisocial behavior, have high self-efficacy, and are not constrained from engaging in criminal activity in the presence of an opportunity and antisocial peers.

Andrews and Bonta's (2003) research explored the relationship between attitudes, including antisocial attitudes, and an individual's inclination towards criminal activity. They identified five elements that constitute an antisocial pattern of attitudes, including a high tolerance for deviance in general, rejection of legal authority and institutions, use of cognitive distortions to justify antisocial behavior, interpretation of a wide range of environmental stimuli as a reason for anger, and a generally antisocial style of thinking. These findings indicate how attitudes can significantly influence an individual's likelihood to engage in criminal behavior. (Schneider et. al, 2005, p.262).

Upon closer examination of the various biological, sociological, and social psychological theories, it becomes clear that no single perspective can fully explain why crimes are committed or why people engage in criminal activities. These three factors are interconnected since an individual's biological makeup is influenced by various genes that predispose them to specific conditions such as mental health and testosterone levels.

Sociological factors also play a significant role, as an individual's learning and nurturing environment is largely determined by their family's socio-economic status and location. Finally, social psychological theories examine an individual's social interactions and their desire to belong to a group, whether it is productive or antisocial. All of these factors, genetics, society, and people, work together to shape an individual's attitudes and propensity to commit crimes and engage in criminal activities..

The Roots of Crime: Examining the Complex Interplay of Biological, Sociological, and Social Psychological Factors.

The movie "Grid Iron Gang" is a story about a juvenile delinquent facility where the leader uses football to rehabilitate the occupants, who are members of rival gangs. In this facility, boys who would typically shoot each other on sight because of their affiliation with rival gangs are given the opportunity to come together and work as a team. Through this process, they learn valuable life lessons and gain new perspectives on acceptable social behavior. In this rewrite, we will explore the plot of the movie, focusing on the key themes of team building, leadership, and social change.

Grid Iron Gang: Using Football as a Tool for Rehabilitation

In the movie Grid Iron Gang, a juvenile delinquent facility uses football to rehabilitate the occupants, who belong to rival gangs that would typically shoot each other on sight, even if they do not know each other but recognize their affiliation.

The Story of a Young Bully

One young man at the center of the story was a bully who initially did not have access to the program. However, he was eventually allowed to join when he reduced his deviant actions. The team members were initially reluctant to join because of their enmity, but they eventually did.

The Power of Teamwork

During one training session, when the boys practiced until they were beyond thirst and were denied water, one guy decided he would not practice anymore. The others agreed with him and sat out the practice. This behavior was not punished but was rewarded as the leaders realized that these rival gang members had done their first action as a team. They soon began to defend and protect each other and showed leadership, determination, and more acceptable social behaviors.

Positive Changes in Attitude and Behavior

Despite having committed various crimes, the boys learned the rules and lessons of being on a team together, where they had to depend on each other for success. They started to change and two boys from rival communities even began to protect each other both in the game and from their own gang members.

Overall, the movie Grid Iron Gang portrays how football can be used as a tool for rehabilitation, especially among juveniles who have committed crimes. The power of teamwork and the positive changes in attitude and behavior can be transformative and life changing.

The Role of Applied Social Psychology in Criminal Investigations and Prosecutions

After a criminal act has been committed, the criminal justice system comes into action in order to bring the perpetrator to justice. The initial step is typically a police investigation, which involves identifying and interviewing potential witnesses and suspects, as well as collecting evidence to support a strong case that can lead to a successful conviction in court.

The aim of applied social psychology in this process is to aid in the development of procedures and guidelines that can improve the efficiency and effectiveness of the investigation (McLeod, 2017).

Police Investigation

To determine whether a crime has taken place, the police must conduct a careful and systematic examination of the scene in order to substantiate and prove that a crime has occurred. This process can be complex and challenging, as it involves ensuring that witnesses, victims, and suspects are interviewed appropriately, and that evidence is collected in accordance with the law (Schneider, 2005). This is essential in order to ensure that the case is held up in court.

Various factors can influence the accuracy and integrity of police work, including biases and errors in investigation procedures. Social psychological theory and research have played significant roles in identifying these potential sources of bias and developing procedures to increase the accuracy and integrity of police officers' work (Wells et al., 2000). For example, social psychology has contributed to the development of procedures for conducting investigative interviews and constructing police line-ups, which are crucial components of criminal investigations (McLeod, 2017).

Overall, the application of social psychology to the criminal justice system has the potential to improve the accuracy and efficiency of investigations and increase the likelihood of successful convictions. By identifying sources of bias and developing evidence-based procedures, social psychology can help ensure that justice is served fairly and accurately.

Enhancing the Accuracy of Police Investigations

Social psychology has played a significant role in identifying possible sources of bias and error in police investigations and developing procedures for increasing the accuracy and integrity of police officers' work. This is important because police officers face undue pressure to conduct investigations in accordance with the law and police procedures.

The practical utility of social psychological research has been to assist police in guarding against systematic biases that may invalidate their investigations and in applying empirically valid procedures. For example, research has contributed to improving the effectiveness of police interviewing procedures by identifying how the social dynamics of the interview environment can influence the efficacy of the interview and how the behavior of the interviewer can impact the behavior of the interviewee.

Furthermore, social psychological research has helped to develop procedures for constructing police line-ups to reduce the likelihood of wrongful convictions. Overall, social psychological research has played a crucial role in improving the accuracy and reliability of police investigations, which ultimately leads to fairer outcomes in the criminal justice system. (Wells et al., 2000)

Police Interviews

Police interviews are a crucial part of criminal investigations as they involve obtaining accurate and credible information from witnesses, victims, and possible suspects. Social psychology has contributed significantly to improving the effectiveness of police interviewing procedures by identifying possible sources of bias and error and developing procedures for increasing the accuracy and integrity of police officers' work.

Creating a Psychological Environment

According to Loe (1992), it is essential for investigators to create a psychological environment that facilitates confession. This involves considering how interviews can be conducted to elicit the most detailed, complete, and accurate information while considering that the atmosphere for each situation is different.

Social Dynamics

The social dynamics of the interview environment can significantly influence the efficacy of the interview. For instance, the behavior of the interviewer can change the behavior of the interviewee. For example, a fidgety investigating officer may cause the interviewee to become restless. This behavior is in keeping with the notion of interactional synchrony, which is the tendency of people to coordinate their body movements during conversation.

Interpretation of Behavior

In situations where the aim is to gather evidence to either support or refute a case, fidgetiness may be interpreted by the investigating officer as signs of deception or guilt, causing the officer to become suspicious. Therefore, it is crucial for investigators to be aware of how their behavior and the interview environment can impact the interviewee's behavior and responses.

Identifying Factors Affecting the Interview Process

Effective police interviews are crucial in obtaining accurate information from witnesses, victims, and suspects. Applied social psychological research has identified key variables that can distinguish productive interviews from unproductive ones. However, common errors such as asking closed-ended questions, interrupting witnesses, and asking leading questions can hinder the effectiveness of the interview.

Police officers with a background knowledge in psychology can identify social and environmental factors that may make a suspect vulnerable during the interviewing process. Additionally, it can help investigators identify their biases and control their perception of innocence or guilt prior to the interview. It is essential for officers to keep the interview environment as neutral as possible to avoid any possible implications.

Police interviewing procedures are an integral part of any criminal investigation. Interviewing witnesses, victims, and suspects can provide valuable information that may help solve a case. However, these procedures are not foolproof and may be subject to biases and errors that could affect the accuracy and integrity of the investigation.

Key Variables to Distinguish Productive Interviews from Unproductive Ones

Applied social psychological research has identified key variables to aid in distinguishing productive interviews from unproductive ones. Common errors that can occur in such interviews include asking too many closed-ended questions, asking too few open-ended questions, interrupting witnesses, and asking leading questions. It is therefore essential that investigating officers have background knowledge in psychology to identify possible social and environmental factors that may make a suspect vulnerable during the interviewing process.

Employing Good Interviewing Techniques

An investigating officer who has been properly trained and exposed to social psychology will be able to employ all the techniques of a good interview, which includes asking simple non-leading questions, using strategic silence, and continuing to reevaluate the working hypotheses in light of new information. Paraphrasing and follow-up questioning may also help to build trust and rapport, providing the best opportunity for the investigating officer to obtain additional and accurate information about the incident while carrying out the careful systematic procedures of the law.

Creating the Right Environment for Each Interviewee

Applied social psychology can assist investigating officers in creating the right environment to suit the needs of each interviewee, whether it be the victim, witness, or suspect, while taking into consideration the gender, age, intelligence, and mental state of each. By creating a psychological environment that will facilitate the act of confessing and avoiding biases, the officer can elicit the most detailed, complete, and accurate information possible.

Applied social psychology has played a significant role in improving police interviewing procedures. By identifying possible sources of bias and error in investigating and developing procedures for increasing the accuracy and integrity of police officers' work, social psychology has provided practical utility in assisting police in guarding against systematic biases that may invalidate their investigations.

Line-up Identification

Identification of suspects is a crucial aspect of any criminal investigation as it provides important evidence for building a case for prosecution. However, it is also a critical area that requires great care to minimize errors in witness judgments. In this regard, social psychological research has played a significant role in identifying factors that influence the accuracy of witness identification procedures.

Reducing Eyewitness Errors through Improved Line-up Procedures

According to Schneider (2005), there is a need to develop line-up identification procedures that reduce eyewitness errors, including the serious problem of false identifications. Social psychological research has shown that witnesses are more susceptible to making errors in judgments under certain circumstances. As such, great care should be taken to minimize these errors.

Factors that Influence Witness Identification Accuracy

Studies have shown that witnesses tend to make fewer mistakes when the perpetrators have distinctive facial features compared to ordinary looking faces. Additionally, identification accuracy is higher when the perpetrators are of the same gender or race as the witness. Moreover, witnesses can attend to the perpetrators' entire face rather than selected features to improve identification accuracy.

Applied social psychology can provide valuable insights into the factors that influence witness identification accuracy. Developing line-up identification procedures that consider these factors can help minimize errors in witness judgments, thereby improving the reliability of evidence in criminal investigations.

Reducing Eyewitness Misidentification

Eyewitness identification plays a critical role in criminal investigations, but false identification can lead to wrongful convictions. Social psychology research has identified several factors that increase the risk of eyewitness misidentification and has proposed strategies and procedures to minimize these risks.

Selection of Foils

One strategy is to carefully select the foils (suspects) to fit the eyewitness's description, while ensuring that they are not too similar to the perpetrator. This reduces the likelihood of the witness simply choosing the most similar individual, rather than the actual perpetrator.

Informing the Witness

Prior to the line-up exercise, the witness should be told that the suspect may or may not be present. This reduces the pressure to make an identification and can prevent false identifications.

Sequential Line-up

The final step is to conduct the line-up one person at a time, sequentially, rather than all at once. This allows the witness to attend to the entire face of the individual and reduces the risk of misidentification. Additionally, the line-up should be conducted by an officer who has no knowledge of the suspect, to minimize the risk of consciously or unconsciously guiding the witness.

Implementing these strategies can help reduce the risk of false identification and ensure that eyewitness testimony is more reliable and accurate in criminal investigations.

The Courtroom

In the context of the adversarial model within a courtroom, it is important to consider the two opposing sets of lawyers, namely the defense and prosecutor. In addition, it is crucial to consider factors such as how they present their arguments, the manner in which they question witnesses, how they build their case before a judge and/or jury, and who ultimately determines the defendant's innocence or guilt.

Defense Lawyers

There are factors to consider for defense lawyers. In the adversarial model of the courtroom situation, defense lawyers play a crucial role in representing the interests of the defendant. To effectively present their case and argue for their client's innocence, defense lawyers need to take into consideration various factors.

Development of a Strong Defense Strategy

A defense lawyer should work closely with their client to develop a strong defense strategy that includes identifying the strengths and weaknesses of the prosecution's case and anticipating potential challenges that may arise during the trial.

Cross-Examination of Prosecution Witnesses

Effective cross-examination of witnesses by the prosecution can help to discredit their testimony and create reasonable doubt in the minds of the jury or judge. Defense lawyers should carefully analyze witness statements and identify inconsistencies or contradictions that can be used to undermine their credibility.

Presentation of Evidence

The defense lawyer should identify and present evidence that supports the defendant's case and challenges the prosecution's evidence. This includes evidence that may have been overlooked by the prosecution or evidence that undermines the reliability or validity of the prosecution's evidence.

Communication with the Defendant

A defense lawyer must maintain open communication with their client to ensure that they are fully informed of the case's progress and can make informed decisions regarding plea bargaining or accepting a plea deal.

Jury Selection

During the trial, the defense lawyer has the opportunity to participate in the selection of the jury. They should take into consideration factors such as demographics, occupation, and beliefs to ensure that the jury is impartial and has no bias against their client.

Presentation of the Defendant

The defense lawyer must present their client in the best possible light, demonstrating their innocence and mitigating any negative perceptions that may exist. This includes presenting the defendant's character witnesses and challenging any negative characterizations that may have been made by the prosecution.

Prosecutors

Also, prosecutors have various factors to consider. Starting with:

Evidence Gathering

Prosecutors need to gather all the relevant evidence to build a strong case against the defendant. They must ensure that the evidence they present in court is admissible and reliable.

Witness Preparation

Prosecutors need to prepare their witnesses for the trial. They must ensure that their witnesses are credible and can provide accurate testimony.

Opening and Closing Statements

Prosecutors need to deliver strong opening and closing statements that are persuasive and clear. These statements should outline the prosecution's case and explain why the defendant is guilty.

Cross-Examination

Prosecutors must effectively cross-examine the defense's witnesses to challenge their credibility and poke holes in their testimony.

Jury Selection

Prosecutors have the responsibility of selecting a jury that will be unbiased and impartial towards the defendant. They need to ensure that the jury is diverse and representative of the community.

Sentencing

After the verdict is reached, prosecutors may have the opportunity to recommend a sentence for the defendant. They must take into consideration the severity of the crime and the defendant's criminal history.

Application of Social Psychology

Social psychology plays a crucial role in shaping the processes and practices of both the prosecutor and defense lawyer in the courtroom. In this section, we will discuss how social psychology can be applied to improve the performance of these legal professionals.

The Prosecutor's Role

The prosecutor's role is to present the case against the defendant and persuade the judge or jury that the defendant is guilty beyond a reasonable doubt. Social psychology research has highlighted several factors that can influence the effectiveness of the prosecutor's performance.

Use of Visual Aids

Visual aids have been found to enhance the persuasiveness of arguments presented by prosecutors. Research has shown that people are more likely to remember information when it is presented in a visual format than when it is presented in a verbal format alone (Tufte, 2006). Therefore, prosecutors should consider using visual aids such as charts, graphs, and diagrams to illustrate their arguments and evidence.

Persuasion Techniques

The use of persuasion techniques such as storytelling, repetition, and emotional appeals has also been found to enhance the effectiveness of the prosecutor's performance. For example, using emotional appeals such as anger or fear can be effective in persuading the jury to convict the defendant (Pennington & Hastie, 1992). Prosecutors can also use storytelling to make their case more engaging and memorable for the jury.

The Defense Lawyer's Role

The defense lawyer's role is to defend the defendant against the charges brought by the prosecution. Social psychology research has identified several factors that can influence the effectiveness of the defense lawyer's performance.

Building Rapport with the Defendant

Building rapport with the defendant can be critical in the defense lawyer's efforts to present a successful case. Research has shown that people are more likely to trust and cooperate with individuals with whom they have established a positive relationship (Davis et al., 2006). Therefore, defense lawyers should focus on building rapport with their clients by showing empathy, actively listening to them, and treating them with respect.

Cross-Examination Techniques

Cross-examination is critical to the defense lawyer's role in the courtroom. Research has shown that cross-examination can be an effective tool for undermining the credibility of prosecution witnesses (Kassin & Wrightsman, 1985). Defense lawyers should focus on using cross-examination techniques such as leading questions, impeaching witnesses, and pointing out inconsistencies in their testimony.

Overall, social psychology plays a crucial role in shaping the processes and practices of both the prosecutor and defense lawyer in the courtroom. By applying social psychology principles, legal professionals can enhance their effectiveness in presenting cases and persuading judges and juries. These principles should be considered by legal professionals in their efforts to provide effective representation for their clients.

Juries

Social psychologists have conducted numerous studies on the dynamics of the courtroom, including the behavior of jurors. These studies aim to understand the social processes that take place among the lawyers, judges, witnesses, defendants, and jurors within the courtroom..

Jury Size

One important aspect of the jury system is the size of the jury. In the United States, juries are typically composed of either six or twelve individuals who are selected from the community where the crime was committed and summoned to appear for jury duty. The U.S. Supreme Court has ruled that reducing a jury from twelve members to six members does not have adverse effects, as these individuals are still considered equivalent (Williams v. Florida, 1970).

Research has shown that the size of the jury tends to have a greater impact on the deliberation process than on the jury's verdict. A meta-analysis conducted by Saks and Marti (1997) found that larger juries tend to deliberate longer, recall more evidence, and engage in more social interaction than smaller juries.

However, the size of the jury has little impact on the ultimate verdict.

Overall, social psychological research has contributed to a better understanding of the role of jury size in the deliberation process and has informed judicial decisions on the appropriate size of juries in criminal trials..

Jury Deliberation

Social psychologists have conducted research on jury deliberation and the factors that influence it. One study conducted by Davis, et al. (1975) found that a unanimous decision by a jury of 12 took longer to reach than a decision by a 6-person jury. This is due to the need for agreement on the verdict and the discussion of evidence and viewpoints in more depth.

However, for a jury to function as intended, it is crucial for jurors to be freed from any preconceived biases that may hinder their ability to render a fair trial. Therefore, it is essential that jurors strive to be impartial and consider all evidence presented to them in a fair and objective manner. This is supported by the American Bar Association, which emphasizes the importance of impartiality in jury selection and deliberation (American Bar Association, 2019).

Jury Prejudice

In their research on juror prejudice, Vidmar and Schuller (2001) identified four distinct types: interest, specific, generic, and normative prejudice. Interest prejudice occurs when a juror has a personal stake in the outcome of the trial, such as a relationship with someone involved in the case.

Specific prejudice arises when a juror holds beliefs or attitudes that could interfere with their ability to be impartial in a specific case, often due to pre-trial publicity in the media. For example, a juror might be related to someone who is called to testify or might know someone who has been charged with the same offence. Specific prejudice occurs when the juror holds attitudes or beliefs that might interfere with his or her ability to be impartial in a particular case. Specific prejudice might arise from exposure to pre-trial publicity presented in the media that biases the juror's judgment of the case.

Generic prejudice refers to a juror's general attitudes or beliefs that may interfere with their impartial evaluation of evidence, such as racist views. Finally, normative prejudice occurs when a juror believes that there is a strong community sentiment supporting a particular outcome of the case, which may compromise their impartiality in favor of the perceived normative attitude..

Preliminary Examination and Jury Bias

During the preliminary examination, potential jurors who are found to be biased can be removed. However, in high-profile cases that receive extensive media coverage, it may be difficult to find impartial jurors from the community where the crime took place. Additionally, if a member of the jury becomes aware of information that may bias their judgment, such as hearing a rumor or seeing biased information in the media, the trial may need to be adjourned until the prejudicial information becomes less salient.

Function of the Jury

The primary function of the jury is to decide about the guilt or innocence of the defendant beyond a reasonable doubt, based solely on the admissible trial evidence. Solutions such as adjournment due to prejudicial information are rarely used, according to Vidmar and Schuller (2001)..

The Prison Setting

According to the U.S. Department of Justice (2003), only 71% of prisoners in the United States serve their sentences in the community, such as through probation or parole. Each individual has a different perception of prisons; some may view them as harsh, inhospitable, and violent environments where inmates keep to themselves, and the sound of slamming steel doors is a constant reminder of the controlled movement.

There is often a clear hierarchy among the prison population, with the toughest and most respected inmates controlling the social order while sex offenders occupy the lowest rung. Furthermore, some may believe that correctional officers, also known as guards or "screws," either become crooked from working in this coercive environment or contribute to the hostility.

On the other hand, some individuals might have a completely different impression of prisons. They may view them as places where inmates are afforded many privileges and rights, including three meals a day, a bed to sleep in, and access to recreational activities, education, trade skills, and treatment programs (although at a financial cost to them).

While this may be true to some extent in minimum security facilities, or in some cases of maximum-security facilities, the reality is much more complex than these simplistic portrayals. Prisons across North America have varying degrees of social environments ranging from very repressive to more humane.

Purpose

Prisons serve multiple purposes, one of which is to protect society by removing dangerous criminals from the streets. Imprisonment also functions as a form of punishment for the offender's antisocial behavior. Moreover, prisons are intended to rehabilitate inmates, to modify or correct their criminal behavior, and prepare them for reintegration into society.

Additionally, they serve the purposes of denunciation and retribution, sending a message that certain behaviors will not be tolerated and serving as a means of "repaying" society for the harm caused by the offender's criminal actions.

Moos (1987) proposed that the social environment in a correctional facility, such as a prison, jail, detention center, or group home for offenders, is made up of three main dimensions, each of which can be measured by three subscales. The dimensions and subscales are as follows:

- Relationship-Oriented (involvement, support, and expressiveness)
- Personal Development (autonomy, practical orientation, and personal problem orientation)
- System Maintenance and System Change (order and organization, program clarity, and staff control).

These dimensions and subscales help in understanding the social climate within the correctional setting and how it affects the behavior and attitudes of the inmates. For example, a positive social climate that emphasizes support, involvement, and personal development can lead to better outcomes such as reduced recidivism rates, while a negative social climate that emphasizes staff control and order can lead to negative outcomes such as increased violence and aggression among inmates. It is important for correctional facilities to pay attention to the social climate and strive to create a positive and supportive environment for inmates in order to improve outcomes for both inmates and society as a whole.

Types of Prison

There are different types of prisons, including the Stanford Prison simulation and Therapeutic Communities.

Stanford Prison Simulation

In the Stanford Prison simulation, the social climate of a prison is defined by various dimensions that reflect the roles and relationships between staff and inmates. This simulation demonstrated the power imbalance that exists in a correctional setting and its potential for abuse.

Therapeutic Communities

Therapeutic Communities, on the other hand, are based on principles developed by Maxwell Jones, including democratization, communalism, reality confrontation, and peer group influence. These communities provide a holistic residential environment that promotes personal growth and development of the residents. The primary aim is to bring about changes in attitudes, beliefs, and behaviors that lead to a healthier and more adaptive lifestyle upon returning to the community.

The core concept of a therapeutic community is living and learning, adhering to the principles of honesty, openness, self-governance, and learning from individuals' efforts to live together. The community is the primary vehicle for promoting social and psychological change, distinguishing it from other therapeutic approaches. A prison-based therapeutic community is built on the idea that prisons are microcosms of the larger coercive and maladaptive environments that inmates often inhabit. Therefore, therapeutic communities provide a structured setting that models a cooperative, prosocial environment..

("Sept 17th 2019.docx - PSYCHOLOGY APPLIED TO THE LEGAL...")

Attributes of Prison Workers

The physical and psychological attributes of those who work in the criminal justice system play a critical role in their ability to perform their duties effectively. The US Department of Labor has established rigorous physical and personal qualifications that candidates must meet.

Interpersonal Skills

Police, detectives, and special agents have the responsibility to enforce the law and departmental rules, although they work independently. It is important for candidates to possess interpersonal skills and enjoy working with the public.

Prison workers must be able to build positive relationships with inmates and colleagues. This requires strong interpersonal skills, including empathy, active listening, and the ability to establish rapport with others.

Honesty and Integrity

Personal characteristics such as honesty, judgment, integrity, and a sense of responsibility are especially important in the field of law enforcement. Senior officers interview candidates and conduct background investigations to ensure that candidates possess the necessary character traits to perform effectively in this high-stress career and produce results.

Emotional Stability

Prison workers are often exposed to traumatic situations and must be able to remain calm and level-headed in the face of challenging circumstances. They must also be able to maintain their composure when dealing with difficult inmates.

Cultural Competency

Prison workers must be able to work effectively with individuals from a variety of cultural backgrounds. They should understand different cultural norms, values, and beliefs, as well as an ability to communicate effectively with people from diverse backgrounds.

Physical Fitness

Prison workers may be required to engage in physical activities, such as restraining inmates or responding to emergency situations. Therefore, physical fitness is an important attribute for this role.

Communication Skills

Effective communication is essential in a prison environment. Prison workers must be able to communicate clearly and effectively with inmates, colleagues, and supervisors. They should also be able to de-escalate potentially volatile situations through effective communication.

Ethical Conduct

Prison workers must uphold high standards of ethical conduct and integrity. They should be honest, fair, and impartial in their dealings with inmates and other staff members.

Problem-Solving Skills

Prison workers must be able to think critically and make quick decisions in high-pressure situations. They should be able to anticipate potential problems and develop effective strategies for resolving them.

Flexibility and Adaptability:

Prison workers must be able to adapt to changing circumstances and work effectively in a variety of different situations. They should be able to adjust their approach based on the needs of individual inmates and respond effectively to unexpected challenges.

Criticisms of the System

The criminal justice system has come under scrutiny for various reasons, including instances of corruption, long wait times for cases to be resolved, and a lack of proper rehabilitation for offenders. While law enforcement officers are often viewed as moral upholders of the law, they are still human and capable of falling into immoral behavior. For instance, psychopaths can manipulate tests, so why couldn't they do the same in the justice system?

Lengthy Court Process

The lengthy court process often results in cases going unresolved for years, leaving room for individuals to go undetected if they are corrupt. The training and camaraderie of law enforcement may also allow for small mistakes to go unnoticed, leading to incidents involving drugs, guns, bribery, and extortion.

Juvenile Delinquents

Juvenile delinquents may also fall through the cracks of the system, either by not receiving proper rehabilitation or by being passed through the system without someone taking notice. Additionally, the cold nature of the system often leaves offenders feeling hopeless, resulting in worsening behavior upon release.

Immoral Court Cases

Unfortunately, cases are sometimes gained immorally in court, with police officers, judges, or lawyers being bought. The lure of money can cause officers of the court to abandon their duty to uphold the law and engage in behaviors such as tampering with evidence or providing incorrect reports. Lawyers are often viewed negatively, and judges may hand down unfair judgments.

Insensitive Behavior

The daily stress and inhumane situations faced by law enforcement can lead to disheartened or insensitive behavior, including racial profiling, a "guilty until proven innocent" mentality, and blaming female victims of sexual assault. Some officers may also become complacent and ride out their careers without seeking to make a difference.

Media as a Whipping Stick

The media plays a significant role in shaping perceptions of the criminal justice system. While it can be a tool for informing the public and putting faces to criminals, it can also be used as a whipping stick. Unfortunately, the criminal justice system cannot prevent all crimes from occurring, which remains a significant limitation.

False Sense of Morality

There is a common perception that law enforcement officers are immune to committing crimes due to their role in upholding the law. However, police officers are human beings who are susceptible to making mistakes and engaging in criminal behavior. This notion is compounded by the fact that psychopaths can manipulate tests to avoid detection. If psychopaths can do so, why can't corrupt officers do the same in the justice system?

Corruption

Corruption is a major issue within the criminal justice system. There is too much room for corrupt officers to go undetected, and the training and comradeship that comes with being a law enforcement officer can allow for mistakes to go unnoticed or brushed under the carpet. This can result in police officers becoming involved in drugs, guns, bribery, extortion, and other illegal activities.

Hopelessness of Rehabilitation

The criminal justice system can be cold and heartless, leading to a lack of hope for rehabilitation or change among those who pass through it. This can result in individuals leaving the system worse off than when they entered it.

Negative Perception of Lawyers

Lawyers are often associated with negative terms such as "sleazy" or "liars." This perception can make it difficult for them to gain the trust of the public or navigate the justice system effectively.

Unfair Judgments

Judges may hand down judgments that are unfair in terms of being either too long or too short. This can lead to a lack of faith in the justice system and its ability to dispense justice equitably.

Negative Attitudes of Law Officers

The daily stress and inhumane situations faced by law enforcement officers can lead to disheartenment and insensitivity. This can result in racial profiling, snap judgments, or not responding to certain calls in some communities until they have no choice. Additionally, some officers may blame or ridicule females when they are victims of rape.

Complacency

Some officers may become complacent, simply waiting for retirement and not seeking to make a difference. This can be seen in media portrayals such as the movie "16 Blocks" with Bruce Willis and Mos Def.

Inability to Prevent Crimes

One major limitation of the criminal justice system is its inability to prevent crimes from occurring. While it can be effective in punishing offenders after the fact, it often falls short in preventing crime in the first place.

Do note that while some of these points may have some validity, it is important to recognize that they do not apply to all law enforcement officers or members of the criminal justice system. It is important to approach these issues with a nuanced understanding and work towards addressing them through meaningful reform and change.

Positives of Social Psychology

The criminal justice system involves a range of professionals who rely on the principles of psychology to improve their effectiveness and accuracy. Police officers and investigators, for example, develop interviewing techniques that draw on psychological research to improve the accuracy and reliability of their investigations. They learn how to avoid potential sources of bias and error in carrying out their work and develop procedures to increase the accuracy and integrity of their investigations.

Improving Investigations

The principles of social psychology can assist law enforcement officers in conducting more thorough and effective investigations. For example, the Reid Technique is an interviewing method used by police officers to extract confessions from suspects. This method uses social psychological principles such as rapport building, cognitive interviewing, and persuasive techniques to elicit truthful information from suspects (Gudjonsson & Pearse, 2011). Additionally, the use of cognitive interviewing has been shown to be an effective way to improve the accuracy and completeness of eyewitness testimony (Fisher & Geiselman, 1992).

Promoting Rehabilitation

Social psychology has been instrumental in promoting rehabilitation and reducing recidivism rates among offenders. Research shows that interventions based on social learning theory have been effective in promoting positive behavior change among offenders (Andrews & Bonta, 2010). Cognitive-behavioral therapy (CBT), which is based on social learning theory, has been effective in reducing recidivism rates among offenders with substance abuse problems (Peters & Murrin, 2000).

Reducing Recidivism Rates

Recidivism rates are a significant concern in the criminal justice system. Social psychology has played a role in developing programs that reduce the likelihood of reoffending. For example, restorative justice programs are designed to help offenders take responsibility for their actions and make amends for the harm they have caused (Braithwaite, 2002). ("[Solved] Provides one example of any feature in the correctional ...") These programs have been shown to reduce recidivism rates among offenders by promoting empathy and reducing hostility towards victims (Sherman & Strang, 2007).

Assisting Defense Attorneys

Assisting defense attorneys is another area where social psychology plays a vital role. Defense attorneys rely on psychological expertise to demonstrate how a person can come to be wrongly accused of a crime and to provide possible explanations for why an individual may have been driven to commit a crime. This helps them to build a more compelling case in court.

Improving Jury Selection

The use of psychological principles also extends to jury selection, where lawyers use their knowledge of human behavior and cognition to identify potential biases and prejudices among prospective jurors. Forensic psychologists, on the other hand, use psychological assessments and risk assessments to predict the probability of future criminal behavior and develop appropriate interventions.

Social learning theory, as posited by Bandura, provides insight into why people commit crimes and how they can be rehabilitated. This theory suggests that individuals learn behaviors through their interactions and experiences in their social environment. For example, juvenile detention centers use rules and shared experiences to deter repeat offenses and promote positive behaviors.

Identifying Sources Of Bias And Error

Finally, psychology plays a critical role in identifying sources of bias and error in the investigative process and developing procedures to increase accuracy and integrity. For example, police investigators learn to avoid fidgeting during interviews to avoid influencing the interviewee's behavior.

Overall, social psychology plays an integral role in various aspects of the criminal justice system, from investigating crimes to rehabilitating offenders. By applying psychological principles and theories, professionals in the criminal justice system can improve the accuracy, fairness, and effectiveness of their work. It can also improve the lives of offenders and victims alike.

Conclusion

Psychology plays a crucial role in the criminal justice system, as it helps professionals understand why people behave in deviant ways and how they can be rehabilitated and reintegrated into society. According to a report by the American Psychological Association, psychology has been applied in various areas of criminal justice, such as policing, corrections, and the courts, to promote fairness, effectiveness, and public safety.

In the courts, for example, forensic psychologists provide expert testimony to help judges and juries understand the mental state of defendants and their ability to stand trial. In juvenile detention centers and prisons, psychologists provide counseling and treatment to address the underlying issues that lead to criminal behavior and help individuals develop the skills and mindset needed to become productive members of society.

Several theories have been proposed to explain criminal behavior, such as the cognitive dissonance theory, which suggests that individuals may experience psychological discomfort when their behavior contradicts their beliefs, and the subculture theory, which posits that criminal behavior may be influenced by the norms and values of a particular group or community.

Moreover, the field of criminal justice examines the nature of crime and the various agencies and processes involved in preventing and addressing it. Students of criminal justice are exposed to critical thinking about ethical considerations related to issues such as the death penalty, drug and gun trafficking, and murder. They also learn how to evaluate the effectiveness of different interventions and strategies aimed at reducing crime rates.

In conclusion, psychology and criminal justice are intertwined, and the application of psychological principles and theories can help improve the effectiveness and fairness of the criminal justice system.

References

1. (2007). International journal of psychology. Retrieved from http://www.tandf.co.uk/journals/titles/00207594.asp

2. (2007). North American journal of psychology. Retrieved from http://najp.8m.com/

3. Andrews, D. A., & Bonta, J. (2010). Rehabilitating criminal justice policy and practice. Psychology, Public Policy, and Law, 16(1), 39-55.

4. Arkin, R. (2007). Basic and applied social psychology. Department of Psychology. The Ohio State University, Columbus, OH. Retrieved from http://www.basp.osu.edu/

5. Braithwaite, J. (2002). Restorative justice and responsive regulation. Oxford University Press.

6. Brody, J. (2002). David Rowe counts teeth. Human Nature Review. 2: 224-228. Retrieved from http://human-nature.com/nibbs/02/rowe.html

7. Campbell, A. (1999). Staying alive: Evolution, culture, and women's intrasexual aggression. Behavioral and Brian Sciences, 22:203-214.

8. Clark, T. W. (2003). Against retribution. A review of placing blame: A general theory of criminal law by Michael Moore. Human Nature Review. 3: 466-479. Retrieved from http://human-nature.com/nibbs/03/twclark.html

9. Darwin, C. (2005). The descent of man chapter IV. Comparison Of The Mental Powers Of Man And The Lower Animals (Continued). Retrieved from http://www.human-nature.com/darwin/descent/chap4.htm

10. Davis, M. H., Conklin, L., Smith, A., & Luce, C. (2006). Effect of perspective taking on the cognitive representation of persons: A merging of self and other. Journal of Personality and Social Psychology, 90(4), 677-688.

11. Fisher, R. P., & Geiselman, R. E. (1992). Memory-enhancing techniques for investigative interviewing: The cognitive interview. Charles C. Thomas Publisher.

12. Gudjonsson, G. H., & Pearse, J. (2011). Suspect interviews and false confessions: A review of the literature. Psychiatry, Psychology and Law, 18(2), 209-222.

13. Haralan, A. (2005). What is emerging in the newly-emerging democracies? The case of Bulgaria: A critique. Retrieved from http://human-nature.com/hraj/harry.html

14. Hare, R.D. (1993). Without conscience: The disturbing world of the psychopaths among us. New York, NY: Simon and Schuster.

15. Kassin, S. M., & Wrightsman, L. S. (1985). The psychology of evidence and trial procedure. Beverly Hills, CA: Sage.

16. Laakso, M. Vaurio, O. Koivisto, E. Savolainen, et al. (2001). Psychopathy and the posterior hippocampus. Behavioural Brain Research. 118: 187-93.

17. Lipton, J. E. (2003). Review of the tending instinct: How nurturing is essential to who we are and how we live by Shelley E. Taylor. Human Nature Review. 3: 44-46. Retrieved from

http://human-nature.com/nibbs/03/taylor.html

18. McLeod, S. A. (2017). Applied psychology. Simply Psychology.

19. Moffitt, T. (1993). Adolescent-limited and life-course-persistent antisocial behavior: A developmental taxonomy. Psychological Review, 100:674-701

20. Penn, D. (2003). On nature and nurture. A Review of Nature Via Nurture: Genes, Experience, and What Makes Us Human by Matt Ridley. Human Nature Review. 3: 461-465. Retrieved from http://www.human-nature.com/nibbs/contents.html

21. Pennington, N., & Hastie, R. (1992). Explaining the evidence: Tests of the story model for juror decision making. Journal of Personality and Social Psychology, 62(2), 189-206.

22. Peters, R. H., & Murrin, M. R. (2000). Effectiveness of treatment-based drug courts in reducing criminal recidivism. Criminal Justice and Behavior, 27(1), 72-96.

23. Pitchford, I. (2001). The origins of violence: Is psychopathy an adaptation? Human Nature Review. 1: 28-36. Retrieved from http://human-nature.com/nibbs/01/psychopathy.html

24. Puget, J. (2007). The state of threat and psychoanalysis: From the uncanny that structures to the uncanny that alienates. Retrieved from http://human-nature.com/free-associations/puget.html

25. Schneider, F. W. (2005). Applied social psychology: Understanding and addressing social and practical problems. Thousand Oaks, CA: Sage Publications.

26. Sherman, L. W., & Strang, H. (2007). Restorative justice: The evidence. The Smith Institute.

27. Smith, S. Arnett, P. Newman, J. (1992). Neuropsychological differentiation of psychopathic and nonpsychopathic criminal offenders. Personality & Individual Differences. 13: 1233-1243.

28. Thompson, K. S. (2003). Review of homicide survivors: Misunderstood grievers by Judie A. Bucholz. Human

Nature Review. 3: 329-330. Retrieved from http://human-nature.com/nibbs/03/bucholz.html

29. Tomov, T. (2005). Social violence and the social institutions. Retrieved from http://human-nature.com/hraj/ttsocvi.html

30. Tufte, E. R. (2006). Beautiful evidence. Cheshire, CT: Graphics Press.

31. Wallace, R. (2002). New wave of crime fighters hits air waves. Fox News.com Wednesday, September 25, 2002. Retrieved from http://www.foxnews.com/printer_friendly_story/0,3566,63997,00.html

32. Walsh, A. (2002). Companions in crime: A biosocial perspective. Human Nature Review. 2: 169-178. Retrieved from http://human-nature.com/nibbs/02/walsh.html

33. Walsh, A. (2003). The holy trinity and the legacy of the Italian school of criminal anthropology. Human Nature Review. 3: 1-11. Retrieved from http://human-nature.com/nibbs/03/gibson.html

34. Walsh, A. (2005). The "Why's" of crime and criminality. Human Nature Review. 5: 87-94. Retrieved from http://www.human-nature.com/nibbs/05/awalsh.html

35. Wells, G. L., Memon, A., & Penrod, S. D. (2000). Eyewitness evidence: Improving its probative value. Psychological Science in the Public Interest, 1(2), 45-75.

Acknowledgment

There is one source of wisdom. There is one source of passion. There is one source of strength. There is one source of motivation. There is one source of drive and there is one source from where every dream, vision, and gift flows; that source is God.

Without him, none of this would be possible. It is His guidance, vision, and urging that has made all this possible; the book, Jamaica Pen Publishers, and the dreams from which they came. I honor Him.

To my other support, my twin. You are the oil in my engine, the fire in my heart, the meaning of everything, and the answer to why. I thank you for your encouragement, patience, counsel, and your prayers.

- *Denise N. Fyffe*

Author Bio

Jamaica Pen Publisher's principal author, Denise N. Fyffe, is no stranger to producing books. She has written more than 50 books and continues to inspire new authors through our mentorship program.

Fyffe, as she is often called, grew up in Jamaica and pursued a career in Education, Training, and Software Implementation. A lifelong scholar, Denise often releases fiction and nonfiction content.

Some of her previous works include Thieves in the Workplace, The Caribbean Family, How to Keep Writing, and The Philosophy of Education and Work.

Read more about Denise N. Fyffe on our website at: https://jamaicapenpublishers.com/.

Recommended Books

IS THE REGISTRY HAPPY?
DENISE N. FYFFE

LEARNING MANAGEMENT SYSTEM
EFFICIENCY VS. STAFF
PROFICIENCY
DENISE N. FYFFE

SOPHIE'S PLACE
DENISE N. FYFFE

- 121 -

All books are available at online bookstores, including Amazon.com.

Dear Reader

Thank you for reading this book.

It means so much that you have taken di time out of your busy schedule. Nothing makes us happier than knowing that someone is reading, and hopefully enjoying, what took us many months, even years, to create.

Please stay with us on this journey. We welcome your feedback, opinions, and suggestions about di book. We would appreciate a few lines of review on di website where you purchased this book, or on Amazon.

You can also write us a note at our website Jamaica Pen Publishing on Facebook, or Twitter or contact us at any of our social media accounts.

Jamaica Pen

Printed in Great Britain
by Amazon